This book was created for people who love their pet and have a desire to make them feel extra special. The homemade biscuits are preservative free, veterinarian approved, and most of all, baked
with love,
by you,
for
your
special
friend.

The
bisquits
make
great
gifts for
your friends
and loved
ones pets and
a special treat
for your own
dog. We genuinely
hope that you enjoy

MAIN STREET VETERINARY HOSPITAL
4100 Kirkpatrick Rd. • Flower Mound, TX 75028 • (214) 355-0008

Dear Reader,

Treats can be a fun way to reward your pet for good behavior, and preparing them yourself lets your special friend know how much you care.

Each recipe contained in this book has been reviewed by a veterinarian and found to contain only safe and wholesome ingredients.

While all pets enjoy treats, please remember that these recipes should not be the main source of your pets nutrition and should constitute no more than 10% of your pets diet.

If your pet has special dietary needs, please consult your veterinarian before feeding any treats.

creating these wonderful gifts of love, but most of all, that your pet glows with appreciation and love for the one who put in the extra effort to do something just for him.

Bacon and Eggs Bisquit

Ingredients:

2 cups - Whole wheat flour
1 1/2 cups - Cornmeal
1/2 cup - Bacon (cooked) about 4 to 5 strips
1 cup - Eggs (scrambled) about 3 to 4 eggs
1/4 cup - Vegetable oil
1 cup - Water
1/2 teaspoon - Salt

1. Preheat oven to 350° F.
2. Combine flour, cornmeal, and salt in a large bowl and mix. Add in cooked bacon, cooked eggs, oil , and water. You can also add in some of the bacon grease if desired. Mix thoroughly.
3. Roll dough out onto lightly floured surface to about a 1/2 inch thickness. Cut out bisquits with a cookie cutter (preferably a dog bone shape).
4. Transfer bisquits to an ungreased baking sheet.
5. Bake for 15 to 25 minutes for small (1") or 30 to 35 minutes for large (3") bisquits.
6. Transfer to rack to cool. Store in an airtight container and refrigerate.

Oatmeal Bisquits

Ingredients:

1 1/2 cups - Oatmeal (uncooked)
1 cup - Flour
1 cup - Cornmeal
1 - Egg
1/2 cup - Vegetable oil
1/2 cup - Water
1/2 teaspoon - Salt

1. Preheat oven to 350° F.
2. Combine oatmeal, flour, cornmeal, and salt in a large bowl and mix. Add in egg, oil, and water and mix thoroughly.
3. Roll dough out onto lightly floured surface to about a 1/2 inch thickness. Cut out bisquits with a cookie cutter (preferably a dog bone shape).
4. Transfer bisquits to an ungreased baking sheet.
5. Bake for 15 to 25 minutes for small (1") or 30 to 35 minutes for large (3") bisquits.
6. Transfer to rack to cool. Store in an airtight container and refrigerate.

Lamb and Rice Bisquits

(Great for dogs with sensitive stomachs or allergies)

Ingredients:

1 1/2 cups - Cooked brown rice (white can be used)
1/2 cup- Brown rice (uncooked) white rice can be used
2 cups - Rice flour (to make rice flour grind rice in a food processor until it is a fine powder)
1 pound - Lamb shank
1- Egg
2 Tablespoons - Vegetable oil
1/2 cup - Lamb broth (from cooked lamb shank)
1/2 teaspoon - Salt

1. Boil lamb shank in 4 cups water until thoroughly cooked. Drain and save broth. Cut meat from shank and grind very fine in a food processor. Should yield about 1 cup of lamb meat. Discard bones.
2. Preheat oven to 350° F.
3. Combine rice flour, cooked rice, uncooked rice, lamb meat, and salt in a large bowl, mix. Add in egg, oil, and broth and mix thoroughly.
4. Roll dough out onto lightly floured surface (preferably rice flour) to about a 1/2 inch thickness. Cut bisquits out with cookie cutter (preferably a dog bone shape).
5. Transfer bisquits to an ungreased baking sheet.
6. Bake for 15 to 25 minutes for small (1") or 30 to 35 minutes for large (3") bisquits.
7. Transfer to rack to cool. Store bisquits in an airtight container and refrigerate.

Note: Rice flour can also be found at most health food stores.

7

PEANUT BUTTER BISQUITS

Ingredients:

2 cups - Whole wheat flour
1 cup - Wheat germ
1 cup - Peanut butter
1 - Egg
1/4 cup - Vegetable oil
1/2 cup - Water
1/2 Teaspoon - Salt

1. Preheat oven to 350° F.
2. Combine flour, wheat germ, and salt in a large bowl. Mix in peanut butter, egg, oil and water.
3. Roll dough out onto lightly floured surface to about a 1/2 inch thickness. Cut out bisquits with cookie cutter (preferably a dog bone shape).
4. Transfer bisquits to an ungreased baking sheet.
5. Bake 15 to 25 minutes for small (1") or 30 to 35 minutes for large (3") bisquits.
6. Transfer to rack to cool. Store in an airtight container and refrigerate.

BEEF BISQUITS

INGREDIENTS:

1 CUP - WHOLE WHEAT FLOUR
1 CUP - CORNMEAL
1/2 CUP - WHEAT GERM
1/2 CUP - GROUND BEEF (COOKED)
1/2 CUP - BEEF BROTH
1/2 CUP - VEGETABLE OIL
1 - EGG
1/2 TEASPOON - SALT

1. PREHEAT OVEN TO 350° F.
2. COMBINE CORNMEAL, WHEAT GERM, FLOUR, COOKED GROUND BEEF, AND SALT IN A LARGE BOWL. MIX. ADD IN EGG, OIL, AND BROTH AND MIX THOROUGHLY.
3. ROLL DOUGH OUT ONTO LIGHTLY FLOURED SURFACE TO ABOUT A 1/2 INCH THICKNESS. CUT OUT BISQUITS WITH A COOKIE CUTTER (PREFERABLY A DOG BONE SHAPE).
4. TRANSFER BISQUITS TO AN UNGREASED BAKING SHEET.
5. BAKE FOR 15 TO 25 MINUTES FOR SMALL (1") OR 30 TO 35 MINUTES FOR LARGE (3") BISQUITS. TRANSFER TO RACK TO COOL. STORE BISQUITS IN AN AIRTIGHT CONTAINER AND REFRIGERATE.

NOTE: FOR A LOWER FAT TREAT, TURKEY, CHICKEN OR ANY MEAT OF YOUR CHOICE MAY BE SUBSTITUTED.

Cheese Sticks

INGREDIENTS:

2 CUPS – WHOLE WHEAT FLOUR
1 1/2 CUPS – CORNMEAL
1 CUP – CHEDDAR CHEESE (GRATED)
1 CUP – SWISS CHEESE (GRATED)
1 – EGG
1 CUP – MILK
1/4 CUP – VEGETABLE OIL
1/2 TEASPOON – SALT

1. PREHEAT OVEN TO 350° F.
2. COMBINE FLOUR, CORNMEAL, CHEESES, AND SALT IN A LARGE BOWL , MIX. ADD IN EGG, OIL, AND MILK AND MIX THOROUGHLY.
3. ROLL DOUGH OUT ONTO LIGHTLY FLOURED SURFACE TO ABOUT A 1/2 INCH THICKNESS. CUT IN STRIPS, 1/2 INCH BY 3 INCHES, AND ROLL STRIP TO MAKE ROUND. TAKE TWO STRIPS AND INTERTWINE THEM, PINCH ENDS TOGETHER.
4. TRANSFER INTERTWINED STRIPS TO AN UNGREASED BAKING SHEET.
5. BAKE FOR 30 TO 35 MINUTES.
6. TRANSFER TO RACK TO COOL. STORE IN AN AIRTIGHT CONTAINER AND REFRIGERATE.

DACHSHUND DELIGHTS

Ingredients:

Outer Layer:
2-cups - white flour
1/4 cup - wheat germ
1 - egg
1/2 cup - water

Filling:
1/2 pound ham
1 - egg
1/4 cup - flour
2 tablespoons - cornstarch

Eggwash:
1 - egg white
4 tablespoons - cornstarch

1. Preheat oven to 350° F.

Filling:

2. In medium size bowl, combine ham (chopped very fine in food processor), egg, cornstarch, and flour. Mix thoroughly and set aside.

Outer layer:

3. In large bowl combine flour, wheat germ, egg, and water, mix thoroughly.

4. Roll out outer layer dough onto lightly floured surface about 1/8 to 1/4 inch in thickness. Cut strips in dough about 1 inch by 3 inches.

5. Shape filling, about one teaspoon, into hot dog shape. Place hot dog shaped filling onto an outer layer strip, and roll up until ends meet, seal seam with cornstarch eggwash. Transfer to greased baking sheet. Brush top with more egg wash.

6. Bake for 10 to 15 minutes or until golden. Transfer to rack to cool. Store in an airtight container and refrigerate.

Bacon Bagel Bytes

Ingredients:
1 - Package active dry yeast
3/4 cup -warm water
1/2 Tablespoon - salt
1 - egg white
2 cups - whole wheat flour
4 pieces - bacon (cooked and diced)

1. Dissolve yeast in warm water. Let stand 2 - 3 minutes until bubbles form. Add salt.
2. Add 1 cup flour. Gradually add the other cup of flour while blending, until stiff dough forms.
3. Knead 8 to 10 minutes by hand until smooth, but firm when pinched.
4. Place dough in greased bowl, cover and let rise until it doubles, about one hour.
5. Preheat oven to 450° F.
6. Turn out on floured surface, punch down. Divide dough into 1 inch balls. Let relax 3 to 4 minutes then flatten. Press a finger into center of 1 inch ball and continue through until a ring is formed, shape until a uniform ring is made. Cover and let rise about 10 minutes.
7. Meanwhile, heat 2 quarts water in saucepan. Gently place bagels in simmering water. Simmer each 30 seconds.
8. Remove with slotted skimmer to towel. Place on greased baking sheet. Sprinkle with cornmeal.
9. Brush top with eggwhite wash (eggwhite lightly beaten with water). Sprinkle with bacon bits.
10. Bake 20 to 25 minutes or until a dark golden color.
    Store in airtight container and refrigerate.

Tuna Bisquits

Ingredients:

1 can (8 ounce) - Tuna in oil
2 cups - Cornmeal
2 cups - Flour
3/4 cup - Water
2/3 cup - Vegetable oil
1/2 teaspoon - Salt

1. Preheat oven to 350° F.
2. Drain oil from tuna in can.
3. Combine cornmeal, flour, and salt in a large bowl and mix.
   Add in drained tuna, water, and oil and mix thoroughly.
4. Roll dough out onto lightly floured surface to about a 1/2 inch
   thickness. Cut out bisquits with a cookie cutter (preferably a fish shape).
5. Transfer to an ungreased baking sheet.
6. Bake for 15 to 25 minutes for small (1") or 30 to 35 minutes for large (3")
   bisquits.
7. Transfer to rack to cool. Store in an airtight container and refrigerate.

Liver Chips

Ingredients:

1 pound - Liver (beef or chicken)
1 cup - Whole wheat flour
1 cup - Wheat germ
1 cup - Cornmeal
1/3 cup - Vegetable oil
3/4 cup - Broth from cooked livers
1/2 teaspoon - Salt

1. In a medium sauce pan, cook liver, and liquid liver is in, with two cups water. When liver is fully cooked, remove liver from liquid and set the liquid aside. Grind liver in a food processor until it is a fine paste. Should yield about 1 1/2 cups liver paste.
2. Preheat oven to 350° F.
3. Combine liver paste, flour, wheat germ, cornmeal, and salt in a large bowl, mix. Add in oil and broth and mix thoroughly.
4. Roll dough out onto lightly floured surface to about a 1/4 inch thickness. Cut out chips with round cookie cutter.
5. Transfer chips to an ungreased baking sheet.
6. Bake for 30 to 35 minutes.
7. Transfer chips to rack to cool. Store in an airtight container and refrigerate

Mint Bisquits

Ingredients:
1 cup – Cornmeal
1 cup – White flour
1 cup – Ground beef (cooked)
1/4 cup – Wheat germ
3/4 to 1 cup Fresh mint chopped fine
(dried may be substituted)
1/2 teaspoon – Salt
1 teaspoon – Mint extract (optional)
1 – Egg
1/4 cup – Vegetable oil
1/2 cup – Water

1. Preheat oven to 350° F.
2. Combine cornmeal, flour, salt, ground beef, wheat germ, and mint in a large bowl. Add egg, oil, water, and mint extract and mix thoroughly.
3. Roll dough out on lightly floured surface to about 1/2 inch in thickness. Cut out bisquits with cookie cutter, preferably a dog bone shape.
4. Transfer them to an ungreased baking sheet.
5. Bake for 15 to 25 minutes for small bisquits (1") or 30 to 35 minutes for large (3") bisquits. Transfer to rack to cool. Store in an airtight container and refrigerate.

WHEAT GERM PRETZELS

INGREDIENTS:

2 1/2 CUPS - WHOLE WHEAT FLOUR
1/2 CUP - WHEAT GERM
1 PACKAGE - ACTIVE DRY YEAST
1 - EGG WHITE
2 TABLESPOONS - VEGETABLE OIL
1 TEASPOON - SALT
1 TABLESPOON - ANCHOVY PASTE
1/4 CUP - SWISS OR PARMESAN CHEESE (GRATED)
WATER

1. IN LARGE BOWL, DISSOLVE PACKAGE OF DRY YEAST IN 1 CUP WARM WATER; LET STAND FOR 10 MINUTES.
2. ADD 2 CUPS OF THE FLOUR, SALT AND OIL TO THE YEAST AND WATER MIXTURE. MIX UNTIL SMOOTH, GRADUALLY ADD 1/2 CUP MORE FLOUR TO MAKE A SOFT DOUGH. ADD ANCHOVY PASTE AND MIX OR KNEAD DOUGH UNTIL SMOOTH AND ELASTIC. (YOU MAY HAVE TO ADD UP TO 1/2 CUP MORE FLOUR TO KEEP DOUGH FROM BEING TOO STICKY).
3. PLACE DOUGH IN A GREASED BOWL AND LET RISE IN A WARM PLACE UNTIL IT DOUBLES (45 MINUTES TO AN HOUR).
4. PREHEAT OVEN TO 425 ° F.
5. PUNCH DOUGH DOWN, ADD WHEAT GERM AND DIVIDE INTO 12 EQUAL BALLS. ROLL EACH OUT ON FLOURED SURFACE TO FORM ABOUT AN 18 INCH ROPE. FORM A PRETZEL SHAPE AND TUCK ENDS UNDER.
6. TRANSFER TO GREASED BAKING SHEET. LET RISE UNCOVERED UNTIL PUFFY, (20 TO 25 MINUTES).
7. BRUSH PRETZELS WITH EGG WHITE WASH AND SPRINKLE WITH GRATED CHEESE, (OR HERBS).
8. BAKE UNTIL DARK GOLDEN (12 TO 15 MINUTES). TRANSFER TO RACK TO COOL. STORE IN AN AIRTIGHT CONTAINER AND REFRIGERATE.

CAROB

BOX BONS

Ingredients:
1 package (12 ounce) - Carob chips
1 cup - Peanut butter
1 cup - Wheat germ

1. In double boiler, melt carob chips, stirring continually.
2. Remove from heat and add peanut butter and wheat germ. Stir until mixture thickens enough to form ball in the palm of your hand. (It may be necessary to cool the mixture in the refrigerator).
3. Form balls and roll or sprinkle with wheat germ.
4. Transfer to airtight container and refrigerate.

Note: Do not give your dog chocolate. It is toxic to dogs and hazardous to their health.

Carob may be found at most health food stores.

To: Bridget
From: Sebastian